About the Jesus-Time Journal:

Time with Jesus is so important for C̶_____s but quality time with Jesus
can so easily get neglected. This Jour_____ ___k and keep
you

The Bible section of this journal hel·
think deeper about what you read
website, Jesus-time.o. g.

Pray with confidence when using the prayer section of this journal. The
prompts are based on "The Lord's Prayer" (Matthew 6:9-13). This sets the
tone for a repentant and grateful heart and helps you remember to pray for
others.

The notes section of this journal is good for larger letters to God, lists of
praises, sermon notes, or whatever you want.

Strengthen your Jesus-Time when you use the Jesus-Time Journal everyday!

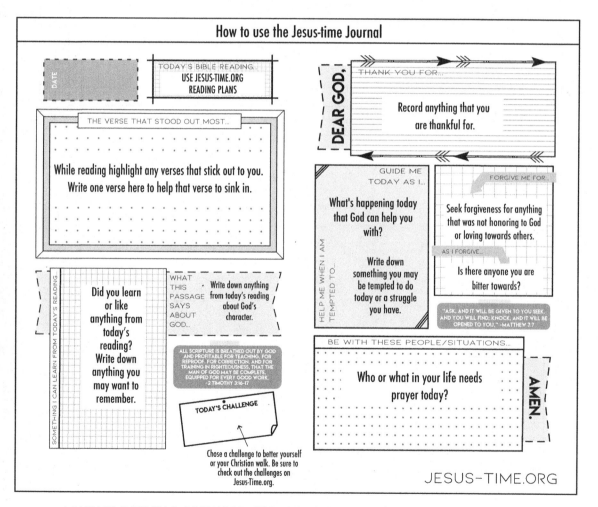

LAYOUT, DESIGN & ARTWORK COPYWRIGHT © 2019 by Susan Ashlee Brower

All bible verses in this book are from the Holy Bible: New International Version. (2011). Grand Rapids, Mich.: Zondervan.

DATE

THE VERSE THAT STOOD OUT MOST...

SOMETHING I CAN LEARN FROM TODAY'S READING...

WHAT
THIS
PASSAGE
SAYS
ABOUT
GOD...

ALL SCRIPTURE IS BREATHED OUT BY GOD AND PROFITABLE FOR TEACHING, FOR REPROOF, FOR CORRECTION, AND FOR TRAINING IN RIGHTEOUSNESS, THAT THE MAN OF GOD MAY BE COMPLETE, EQUIPPED FOR EVERY GOOD WORK.
-2 TIMOTHY 3:16-17

TODAY'S CHALLENGE

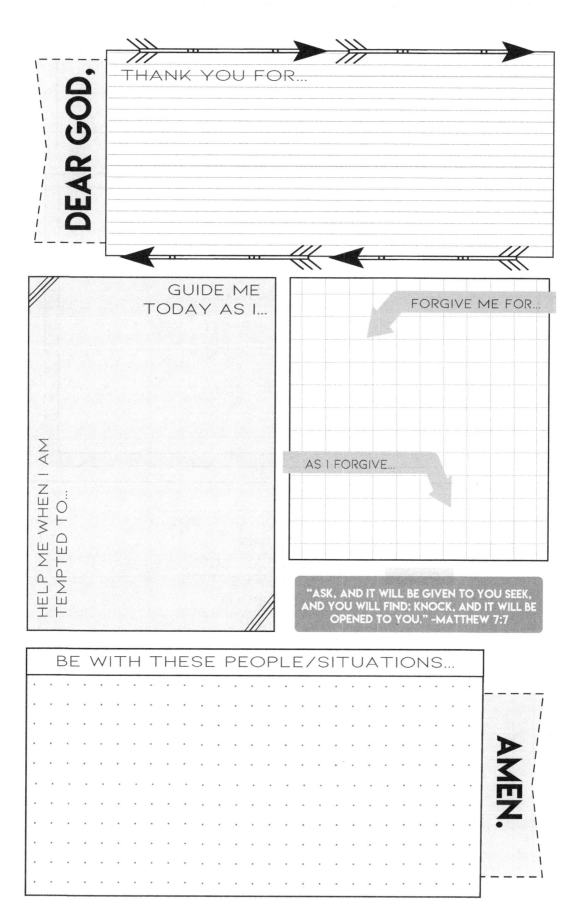

DEAR GOD,

THANK YOU FOR...

GUIDE ME TODAY AS I...

HELP ME WHEN I AM TEMPTED TO...

FORGIVE ME FOR...

AS I FORGIVE...

"ASK, AND IT WILL BE GIVEN TO YOU SEEK, AND YOU WILL FIND: KNOCK, AND IT WILL BE OPENED TO YOU." -MATTHEW 7:7

BE WITH THESE PEOPLE/SITUATIONS...

AMEN.

DATE

TODAY'S BIBLE READING...

THE VERSE THAT STOOD OUT MOST...

SOMETHING I CAN LEARN FROM TODAY'S READING...

WHAT
THIS
PASSAGE
SAYS
ABOUT
GOD...

ALL SCRIPTURE IS BREATHED OUT BY GOD AND PROFITABLE FOR TEACHING, FOR REPROOF, FOR CORRECTION, AND FOR TRAINING IN RIGHTEOUSNESS, THAT THE MAN OF GOD MAY BE COMPLETE, EQUIPPED FOR EVERY GOOD WORK.
-2 TIMOTHY 3:16-17

TODAY'S CHALLENGE

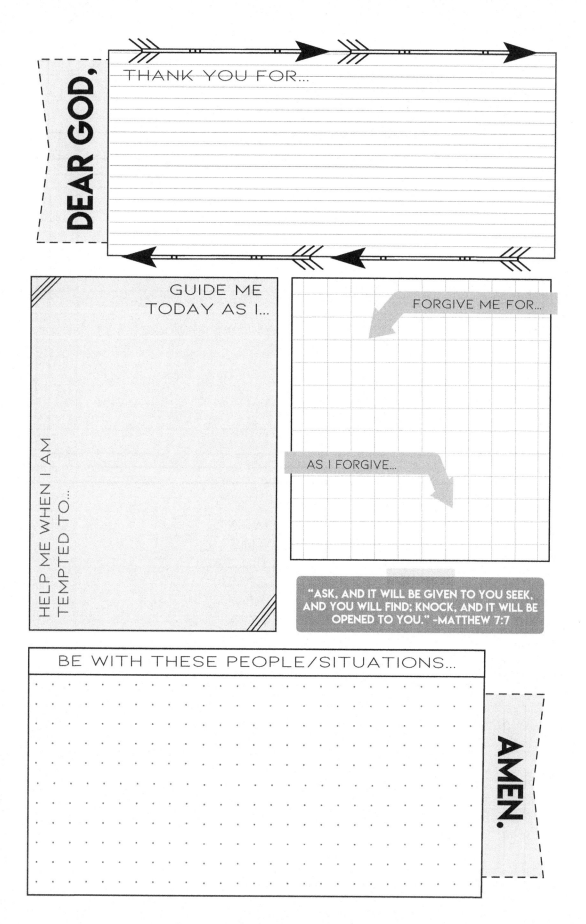

DEAR GOD,

THANK YOU FOR...

GUIDE ME TODAY AS I...

HELP ME WHEN I AM TEMPTED TO...

FORGIVE ME FOR...

AS I FORGIVE...

"ASK, AND IT WILL BE GIVEN TO YOU SEEK, AND YOU WILL FIND; KNOCK, AND IT WILL BE OPENED TO YOU." -MATTHEW 7:7

BE WITH THESE PEOPLE/SITUATIONS...

AMEN.

DATE

TODAY'S BIBLE READING...

THE VERSE THAT STOOD OUT MOST...

SOMETHING I CAN LEARN FROM TODAY'S READING...

WHAT
THIS
PASSAGE
SAYS
ABOUT
GOD...

ALL SCRIPTURE IS BREATHED OUT BY GOD AND PROFITABLE FOR TEACHING, FOR REPROOF, FOR CORRECTION, AND FOR TRAINING IN RIGHTEOUSNESS, THAT THE MAN OF GOD MAY BE COMPLETE, EQUIPPED FOR EVERY GOOD WORK.
-2 TIMOTHY 3:16-17

TODAY'S CHALLENGE

DEAR GOD,

THANK YOU FOR...

GUIDE ME TODAY AS I...

HELP ME WHEN I AM TEMPTED TO...

FORGIVE ME FOR...

AS I FORGIVE...

"ASK, AND IT WILL BE GIVEN TO YOU SEEK, AND YOU WILL FIND; KNOCK, AND IT WILL BE OPENED TO YOU." -MATTHEW 7:7

BE WITH THESE PEOPLE/SITUATIONS...

AMEN.

TODAY'S BIBLE READING...

THE VERSE THAT STOOD OUT MOST...

SOMETHING I CAN LEARN FROM TODAY'S READING...

WHAT
THIS
PASSAGE
SAYS
ABOUT
GOD...

ALL SCRIPTURE IS BREATHED OUT BY GOD AND PROFITABLE FOR TEACHING, FOR REPROOF, FOR CORRECTION, AND FOR TRAINING IN RIGHTEOUSNESS, THAT THE MAN OF GOD MAY BE COMPLETE, EQUIPPED FOR EVERY GOOD WORK.
-2 TIMOTHY 3:16-17

TODAY'S CHALLENGE

DEAR GOD,

THANK YOU FOR...

GUIDE ME TODAY AS I...

HELP ME WHEN I AM TEMPTED TO...

FORGIVE ME FOR...

AS I FORGIVE...

"ASK, AND IT WILL BE GIVEN TO YOU SEEK, AND YOU WILL FIND; KNOCK, AND IT WILL BE OPENED TO YOU." -MATTHEW 7:7

BE WITH THESE PEOPLE/SITUATIONS...

AMEN.

DATE

TODAY'S BIBLE READING...

THE VERSE THAT STOOD OUT MOST...

SOMETHING I CAN LEARN FROM TODAY'S READING...

WHAT
THIS
PASSAGE
SAYS
ABOUT
GOD...

ALL SCRIPTURE IS BREATHED OUT BY GOD AND PROFITABLE FOR TEACHING, FOR REPROOF, FOR CORRECTION, AND FOR TRAINING IN RIGHTEOUSNESS, THAT THE MAN OF GOD MAY BE COMPLETE, EQUIPPED FOR EVERY GOOD WORK.
-2 TIMOTHY 3:16-17

TODAY'S CHALLENGE

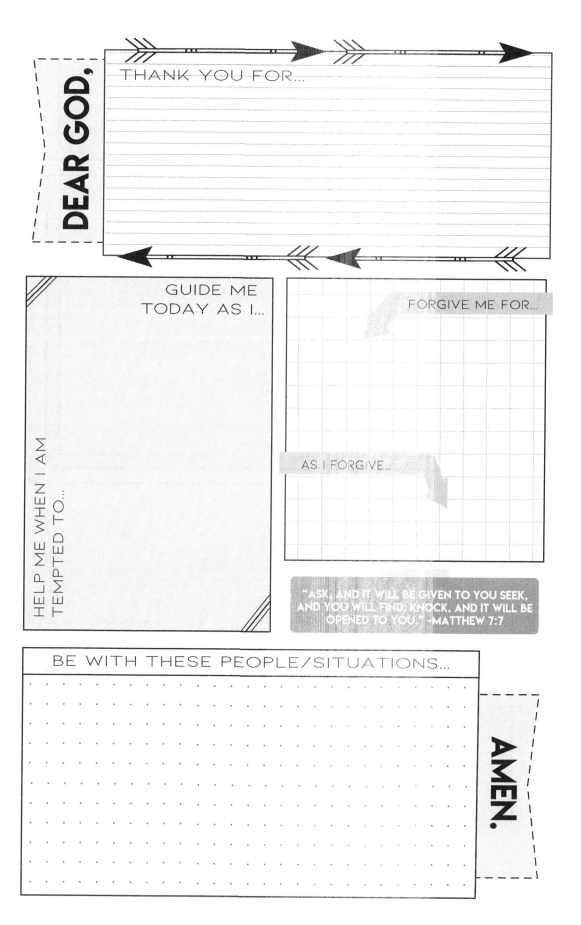

DEAR GOD,

THANK YOU FOR...

GUIDE ME
TODAY AS I...

HELP ME WHEN I AM
TEMPTED TO...

FORGIVE ME FOR...

AS I FORGIVE...

"ASK, AND IT WILL BE GIVEN TO YOU SEEK,
AND YOU WILL FIND; KNOCK, AND IT WILL BE
OPENED TO YOU." -MATTHEW 7:7

BE WITH THESE PEOPLE/SITUATIONS...

AMEN.

TODAY'S BIBLE READING...

THE VERSE THAT STOOD OUT MOST...

SOMETHING I CAN LEARN FROM TODAY'S READING...

WHAT
THIS
PASSAGE
SAYS
ABOUT
GOD...

ALL SCRIPTURE IS BREATHED OUT BY GOD AND PROFITABLE FOR TEACHING, FOR REPROOF, FOR CORRECTION, AND FOR TRAINING IN RIGHTEOUSNESS, THAT THE MAN OF GOD MAY BE COMPLETE, EQUIPPED FOR EVERY GOOD WORK.
-2 TIMOTHY 3:16-17

TODAY'S CHALLENGE

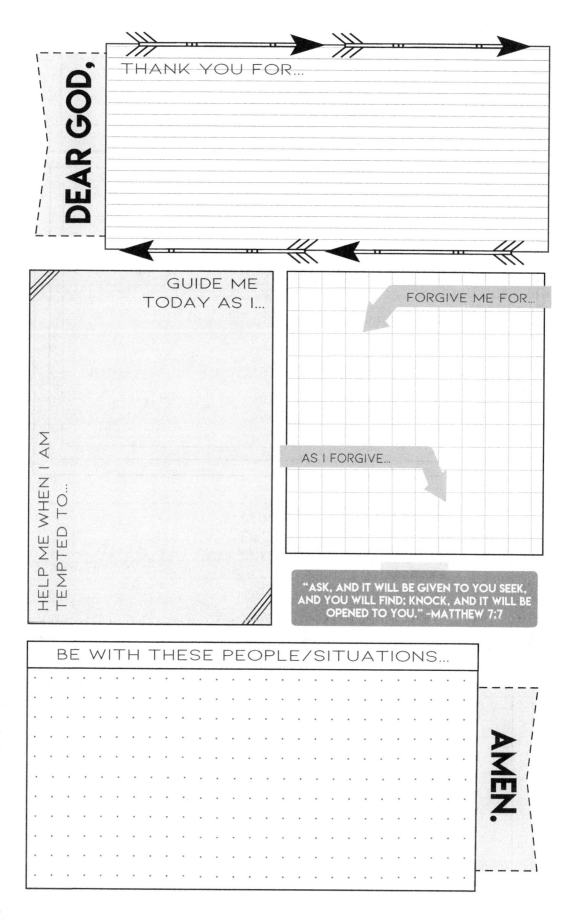

DEAR GOD,

THANK YOU FOR...

GUIDE ME TODAY AS I...

HELP ME WHEN I AM TEMPTED TO...

FORGIVE ME FOR...

AS I FORGIVE...

"ASK, AND IT WILL BE GIVEN TO YOU SEEK, AND YOU WILL FIND; KNOCK, AND IT WILL BE OPENED TO YOU." -MATTHEW 7:7

BE WITH THESE PEOPLE/SITUATIONS...

AMEN.

DATE

TODAY'S BIBLE READING...

THE VERSE THAT STOOD OUT MOST...

SOMETHING I CAN LEARN FROM TODAY'S READING...

WHAT
THIS
PASSAGE
SAYS
ABOUT
GOD...

ALL SCRIPTURE IS BREATHED OUT BY GOD AND PROFITABLE FOR TEACHING, FOR REPROOF, FOR CORRECTION, AND FOR TRAINING IN RIGHTEOUSNESS, THAT THE MAN OF GOD MAY BE COMPLETE, EQUIPPED FOR EVERY GOOD WORK.
-2 TIMOTHY 3:16-17

TODAY'S CHALLENGE

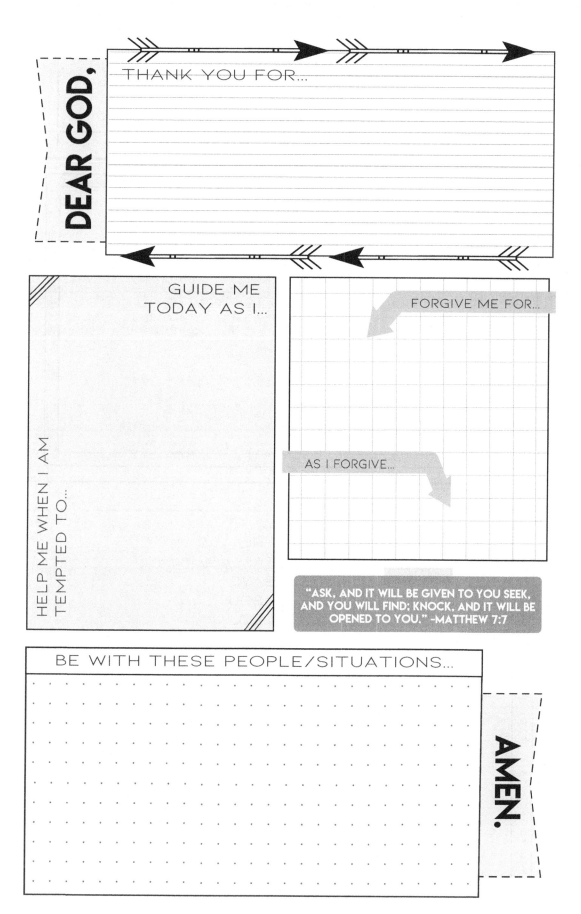

DEAR GOD,

THANK YOU FOR...

GUIDE ME TODAY AS I...

HELP ME WHEN I AM TEMPTED TO...

FORGIVE ME FOR...

AS I FORGIVE...

"ASK, AND IT WILL BE GIVEN TO YOU SEEK, AND YOU WILL FIND; KNOCK, AND IT WILL BE OPENED TO YOU." -MATTHEW 7:7

BE WITH THESE PEOPLE/SITUATIONS...

AMEN.

DATE

TODAY'S BIBLE READING...

THE VERSE THAT STOOD OUT MOST...

SOMETHING I CAN LEARN FROM TODAY'S READING...

WHAT
THIS
PASSAGE
SAYS
ABOUT
GOD...

ALL SCRIPTURE IS BREATHED OUT BY GOD AND PROFITABLE FOR TEACHING, FOR REPROOF, FOR CORRECTION, AND FOR TRAINING IN RIGHTEOUSNESS, THAT THE MAN OF GOD MAY BE COMPLETE, EQUIPPED FOR EVERY GOOD WORK.
-2 TIMOTHY 3:16-17

TODAY'S CHALLENGE

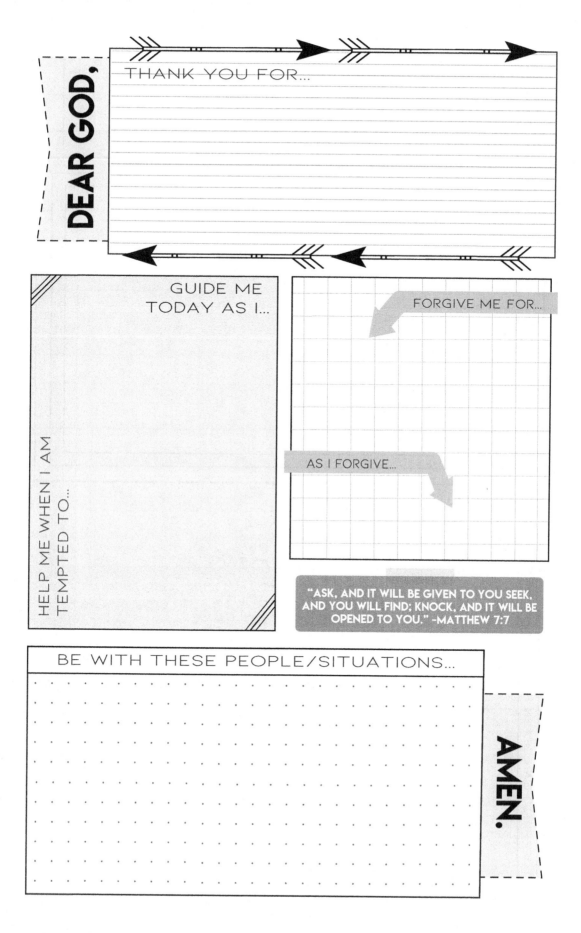

DEAR GOD,

THANK YOU FOR...

GUIDE ME
TODAY AS I...

HELP ME WHEN I AM
TEMPTED TO...

FORGIVE ME FOR...

AS I FORGIVE...

"ASK, AND IT WILL BE GIVEN TO YOU SEEK,
AND YOU WILL FIND; KNOCK, AND IT WILL BE
OPENED TO YOU." -MATTHEW 7:7

BE WITH THESE PEOPLE/SITUATIONS...

AMEN.

DATE

TODAY'S BIBLE READING...

THE VERSE THAT STOOD OUT MOST...

SOMETHING I CAN LEARN FROM TODAY'S READING...

WHAT
THIS
PASSAGE
SAYS
ABOUT
GOD...

ALL SCRIPTURE IS BREATHED OUT BY GOD AND PROFITABLE FOR TEACHING, FOR REPROOF, FOR CORRECTION, AND FOR TRAINING IN RIGHTEOUSNESS, THAT THE MAN OF GOD MAY BE COMPLETE, EQUIPPED FOR EVERY GOOD WORK.
-2 TIMOTHY 3:16-17

TODAY'S CHALLENGE

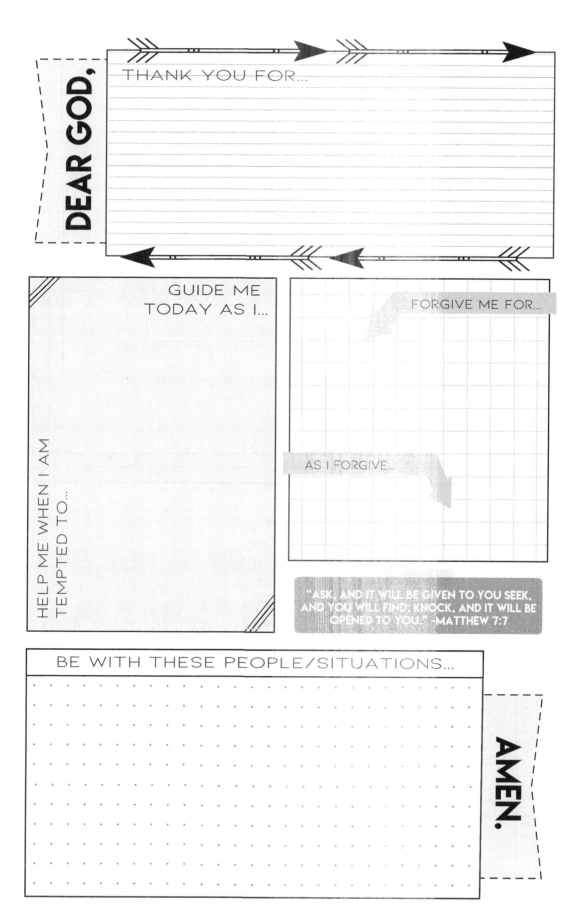

DEAR GOD,

THANK YOU FOR...

GUIDE ME TODAY AS I...

HELP ME WHEN I AM TEMPTED TO...

FORGIVE ME FOR...

AS I FORGIVE...

"ASK, AND IT WILL BE GIVEN TO YOU SEEK, AND YOU WILL FIND; KNOCK, AND IT WILL BE OPENED TO YOU." -MATTHEW 7:7

BE WITH THESE PEOPLE/SITUATIONS...

AMEN.

TODAY'S BIBLE READING...

THE VERSE THAT STOOD OUT MOST...

SOMETHING I CAN LEARN FROM TODAY'S READING...

WHAT
THIS
PASSAGE
SAYS
ABOUT
GOD...

ALL SCRIPTURE IS BREATHED OUT BY GOD AND PROFITABLE FOR TEACHING, FOR REPROOF, FOR CORRECTION, AND FOR TRAINING IN RIGHTEOUSNESS, THAT THE MAN OF GOD MAY BE COMPLETE, EQUIPPED FOR EVERY GOOD WORK.
-2 TIMOTHY 3:16-17

TODAY'S CHALLENGE

DEAR GOD,

THANK YOU FOR...

GUIDE ME
TODAY AS I...

HELP ME WHEN I AM
TEMPTED TO...

FORGIVE ME FOR...

AS I FORGIVE...

"ASK, AND IT WILL BE GIVEN TO YOU SEEK,
AND YOU WILL FIND; KNOCK, AND IT WILL BE
OPENED TO YOU." -MATTHEW 7:7

BE WITH THESE PEOPLE/SITUATIONS...

AMEN.

DATE

TODAY'S BIBLE READING...

THE VERSE THAT STOOD OUT MOST...

SOMETHING I CAN LEARN FROM TODAY'S READING...

WHAT
THIS
PASSAGE
SAYS
ABOUT
GOD...

ALL SCRIPTURE IS BREATHED OUT BY GOD AND PROFITABLE FOR TEACHING, FOR REPROOF, FOR CORRECTION, AND FOR TRAINING IN RIGHTEOUSNESS, THAT THE MAN OF GOD MAY BE COMPLETE, EQUIPPED FOR EVERY GOOD WORK.
-2 TIMOTHY 3:16-17

TODAY'S CHALLENGE

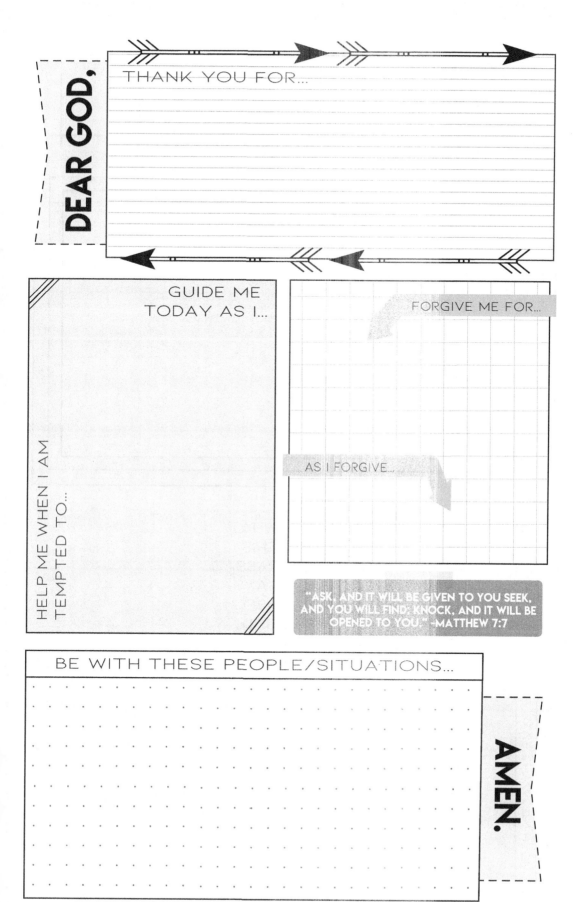

DEAR GOD,

THANK YOU FOR...

GUIDE ME TODAY AS I...

HELP ME WHEN I AM TEMPTED TO...

FORGIVE ME FOR...

AS I FORGIVE...

"ASK, AND IT WILL BE GIVEN TO YOU SEEK, AND YOU WILL FIND; KNOCK, AND IT WILL BE OPENED TO YOU." -MATTHEW 7:7

BE WITH THESE PEOPLE/SITUATIONS...

AMEN.

DATE

THE VERSE THAT STOOD OUT MOST...

SOMETHING I CAN LEARN FROM TODAY'S READING...

WHAT
THIS
PASSAGE
SAYS
ABOUT
GOD...

ALL SCRIPTURE IS BREATHED OUT BY GOD AND PROFITABLE FOR TEACHING, FOR REPROOF, FOR CORRECTION, AND FOR TRAINING IN RIGHTEOUSNESS, THAT THE MAN OF GOD MAY BE COMPLETE, EQUIPPED FOR EVERY GOOD WORK.
-2 TIMOTHY 3:16-17

TODAY'S CHALLENGE

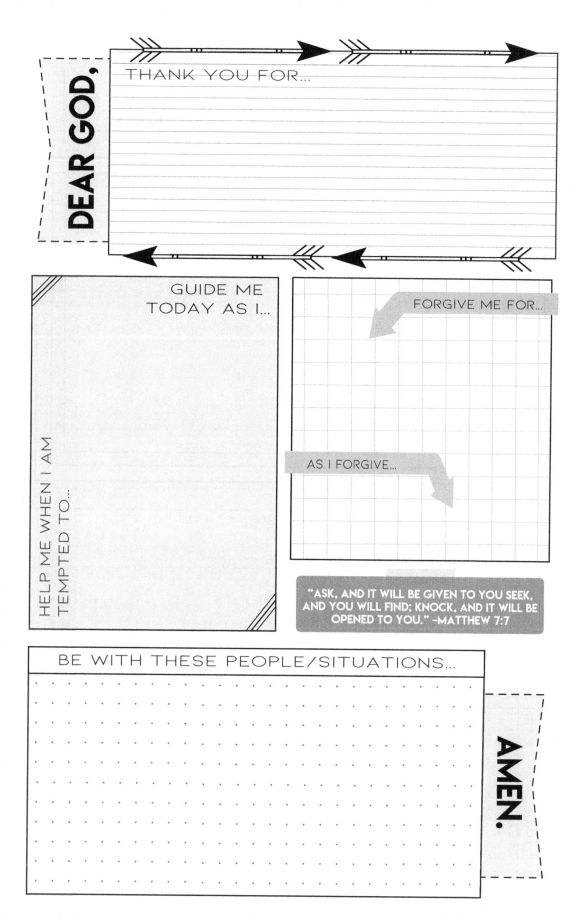

DEAR GOD,

THANK YOU FOR...

GUIDE ME TODAY AS I...

HELP ME WHEN I AM TEMPTED TO...

FORGIVE ME FOR...

AS I FORGIVE...

"ASK, AND IT WILL BE GIVEN TO YOU SEEK, AND YOU WILL FIND; KNOCK, AND IT WILL BE OPENED TO YOU." -MATTHEW 7:7

BE WITH THESE PEOPLE/SITUATIONS...

AMEN.

DATE

TODAY'S BIBLE READING...

THE VERSE THAT STOOD OUT MOST...

SOMETHING I CAN LEARN FROM TODAY'S READING...

WHAT
THIS
PASSAGE
SAYS
ABOUT
GOD...

ALL SCRIPTURE IS BREATHED OUT BY GOD AND PROFITABLE FOR TEACHING, FOR REPROOF, FOR CORRECTION, AND FOR TRAINING IN RIGHTEOUSNESS, THAT THE MAN OF GOD MAY BE COMPLETE, EQUIPPED FOR EVERY GOOD WORK.
-2 TIMOTHY 3:16-17

TODAY'S CHALLENGE

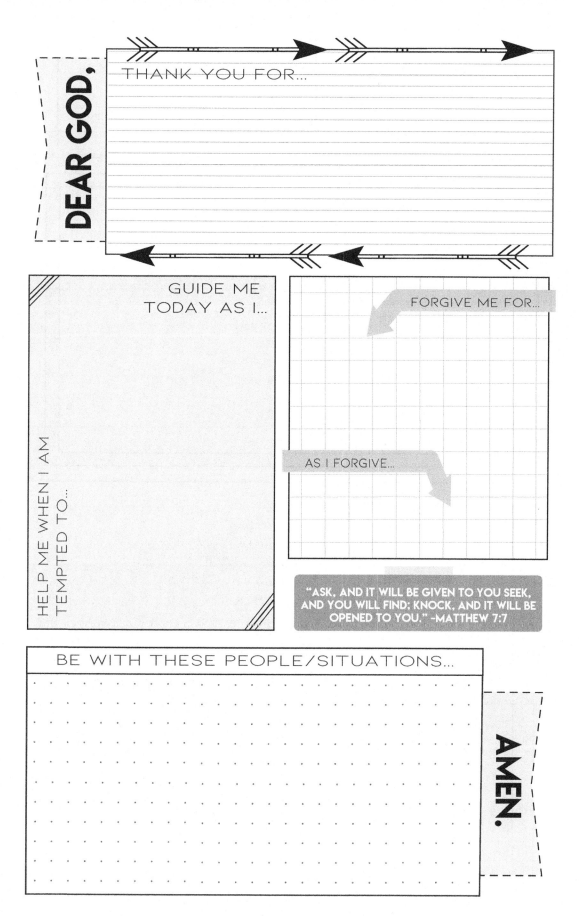

DEAR GOD,

THANK YOU FOR...

GUIDE ME TODAY AS I...

HELP ME WHEN I AM TEMPTED TO...

FORGIVE ME FOR...

AS I FORGIVE...

"ASK, AND IT WILL BE GIVEN TO YOU SEEK, AND YOU WILL FIND; KNOCK, AND IT WILL BE OPENED TO YOU." -MATTHEW 7:7

BE WITH THESE PEOPLE/SITUATIONS...

AMEN.

DATE

TODAY'S BIBLE READING...

THE VERSE THAT STOOD OUT MOST...

SOMETHING I CAN LEARN FROM TODAY'S READING...

WHAT
THIS
PASSAGE
SAYS
ABOUT
GOD...

ALL SCRIPTURE IS BREATHED OUT BY GOD AND PROFITABLE FOR TEACHING, FOR REPROOF, FOR CORRECTION, AND FOR TRAINING IN RIGHTEOUSNESS, THAT THE MAN OF GOD MAY BE COMPLETE, EQUIPPED FOR EVERY GOOD WORK.
-2 TIMOTHY 3:16-17

TODAY'S CHALLENGE

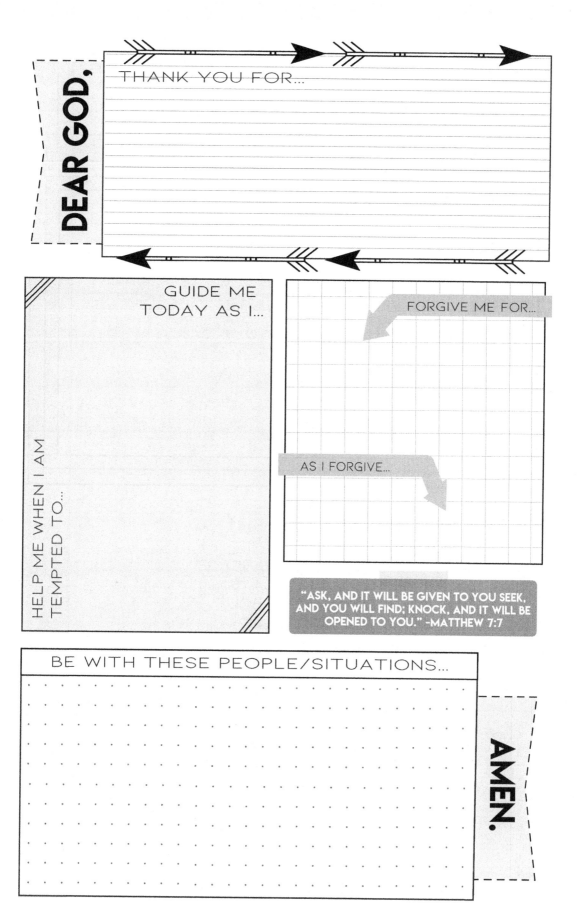

DEAR GOD,

THANK YOU FOR...

GUIDE ME TODAY AS I...

HELP ME WHEN I AM TEMPTED TO...

FORGIVE ME FOR...

AS I FORGIVE...

"ASK, AND IT WILL BE GIVEN TO YOU SEEK, AND YOU WILL FIND; KNOCK, AND IT WILL BE OPENED TO YOU." -MATTHEW 7:7

BE WITH THESE PEOPLE/SITUATIONS...

AMEN.

DATE

TODAY'S BIBLE READING...

THE VERSE THAT STOOD OUT MOST...

SOMETHING I CAN LEARN FROM TODAY'S READING...

WHAT
THIS
PASSAGE
SAYS
ABOUT
GOD...

ALL SCRIPTURE IS BREATHED OUT BY GOD AND PROFITABLE FOR TEACHING, FOR REPROOF, FOR CORRECTION, AND FOR TRAINING IN RIGHTEOUSNESS, THAT THE MAN OF GOD MAY BE COMPLETE, EQUIPPED FOR EVERY GOOD WORK.
-2 TIMOTHY 3:16-17

TODAY'S CHALLENGE

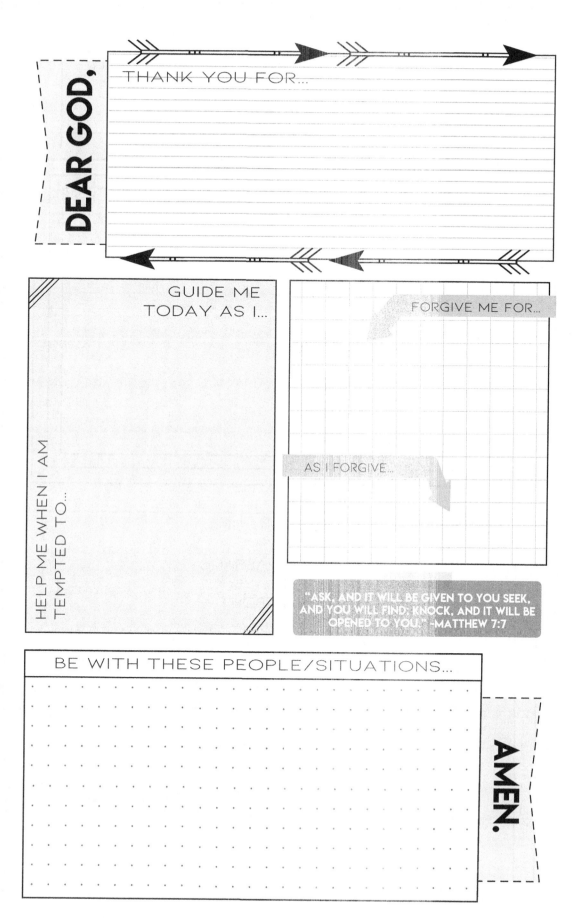

DEAR GOD,

THANK YOU FOR...

GUIDE ME TODAY AS I...

HELP ME WHEN I AM TEMPTED TO...

FORGIVE ME FOR...

AS I FORGIVE...

"ASK, AND IT WILL BE GIVEN TO YOU SEEK, AND YOU WILL FIND; KNOCK, AND IT WILL BE OPENED TO YOU." -MATTHEW 7:7

BE WITH THESE PEOPLE/SITUATIONS...

AMEN.

DATE

TODAY'S BIBLE READING...

THE VERSE THAT STOOD OUT MOST...

SOMETHING I CAN LEARN FROM TODAY'S READING...

WHAT
THIS
PASSAGE
SAYS
ABOUT
GOD...

ALL SCRIPTURE IS BREATHED OUT BY GOD AND PROFITABLE FOR TEACHING, FOR REPROOF, FOR CORRECTION, AND FOR TRAINING IN RIGHTEOUSNESS, THAT THE MAN OF GOD MAY BE COMPLETE, EQUIPPED FOR EVERY GOOD WORK.
-2 TIMOTHY 3:16-17

TODAY'S CHALLENGE

DEAR GOD,

THANK YOU FOR...

GUIDE ME TODAY AS I...

HELP ME WHEN I AM TEMPTED TO...

FORGIVE ME FOR...

AS I FORGIVE...

"ASK, AND IT WILL BE GIVEN TO YOU SEEK, AND YOU WILL FIND; KNOCK, AND IT WILL BE OPENED TO YOU." -MATTHEW 7:7

BE WITH THESE PEOPLE/SITUATIONS...

AMEN.

DATE

TODAY'S BIBLE READING...

THE VERSE THAT STOOD OUT MOST...

SOMETHING I CAN LEARN FROM TODAY'S READING...

WHAT
THIS
PASSAGE
SAYS
ABOUT
GOD...

ALL SCRIPTURE IS BREATHED OUT BY GOD AND PROFITABLE FOR TEACHING, FOR REPROOF, FOR CORRECTION, AND FOR TRAINING IN RIGHTEOUSNESS, THAT THE MAN OF GOD MAY BE COMPLETE, EQUIPPED FOR EVERY GOOD WORK.
-2 TIMOTHY 3:16-17

TODAY'S CHALLENGE

DEAR GOD,

THANK YOU FOR...

GUIDE ME TODAY AS I...

HELP ME WHEN I AM TEMPTED TO...

FORGIVE ME FOR...

AS I FORGIVE...

"ASK, AND IT WILL BE GIVEN TO YOU SEEK, AND YOU WILL FIND; KNOCK, AND IT WILL BE OPENED TO YOU." -MATTHEW 7:7

BE WITH THESE PEOPLE/SITUATIONS...

AMEN.

TODAY'S BIBLE READING...

THE VERSE THAT STOOD OUT MOST...

SOMETHING I CAN LEARN FROM TODAY'S READING...

WHAT
THIS
PASSAGE
SAYS
ABOUT
GOD...

ALL SCRIPTURE IS BREATHED OUT BY GOD AND PROFITABLE FOR TEACHING, FOR REPROOF, FOR CORRECTION, AND FOR TRAINING IN RIGHTEOUSNESS, THAT THE MAN OF GOD MAY BE COMPLETE, EQUIPPED FOR EVERY GOOD WORK. -2 TIMOTHY 3:16-17

TODAY'S CHALLENGE

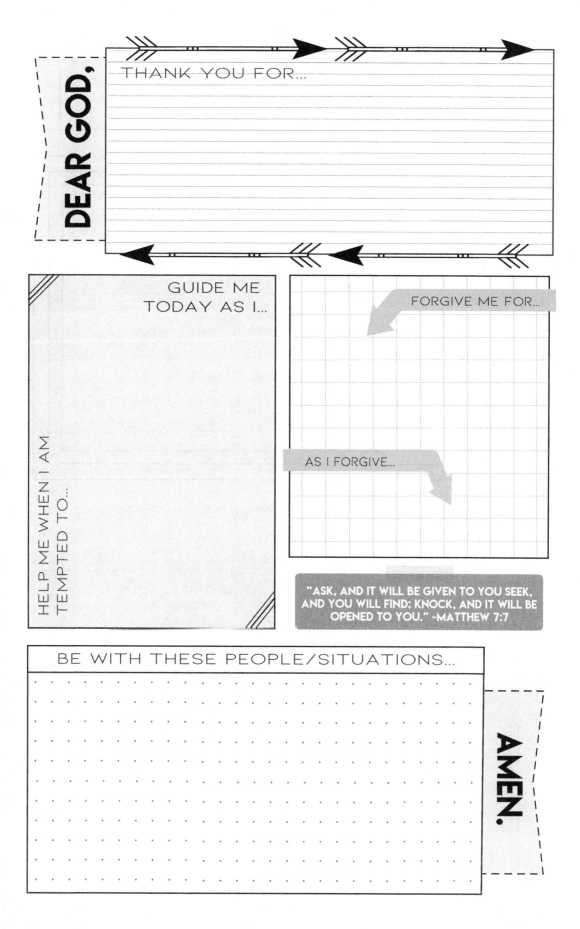

DEAR GOD,

THANK YOU FOR...

GUIDE ME
TODAY AS I...

HELP ME WHEN I AM
TEMPTED TO...

FORGIVE ME FOR...

AS I FORGIVE...

"ASK, AND IT WILL BE GIVEN TO YOU SEEK,
AND YOU WILL FIND; KNOCK, AND IT WILL BE
OPENED TO YOU." -MATTHEW 7:7

BE WITH THESE PEOPLE/SITUATIONS...

AMEN.

DATE

TODAY'S BIBLE READING...

THE VERSE THAT STOOD OUT MOST...

SOMETHING I CAN LEARN FROM TODAY'S READING...

WHAT
THIS
PASSAGE
SAYS
ABOUT
GOD...

ALL SCRIPTURE IS BREATHED OUT BY GOD AND PROFITABLE FOR TEACHING, FOR REPROOF, FOR CORRECTION, AND FOR TRAINING IN RIGHTEOUSNESS, THAT THE MAN OF GOD MAY BE COMPLETE, EQUIPPED FOR EVERY GOOD WORK.
-2 TIMOTHY 3:16-17

TODAY'S CHALLENGE

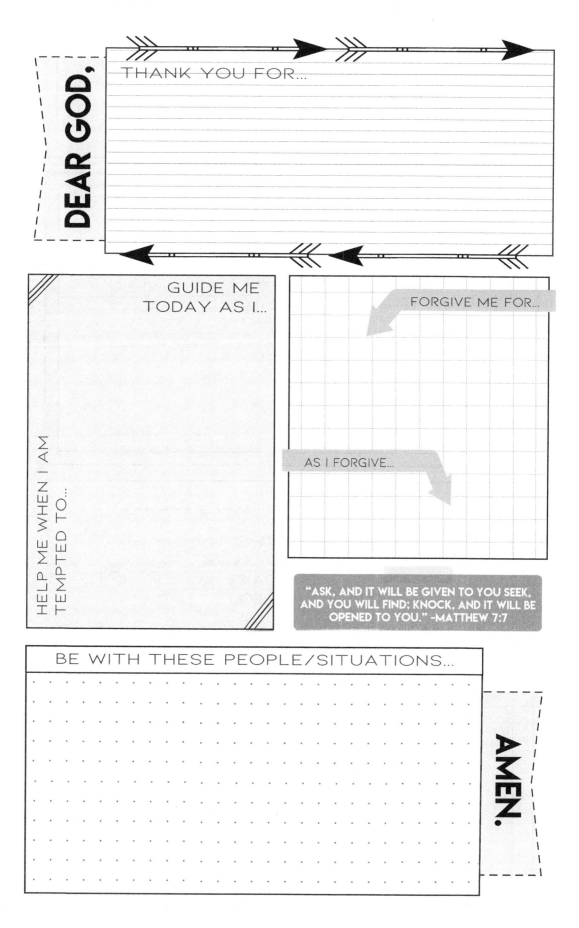

DEAR GOD,

THANK YOU FOR...

GUIDE ME TODAY AS I...

HELP ME WHEN I AM TEMPTED TO...

FORGIVE ME FOR...

AS I FORGIVE...

"ASK, AND IT WILL BE GIVEN TO YOU SEEK, AND YOU WILL FIND; KNOCK, AND IT WILL BE OPENED TO YOU." -MATTHEW 7:7

BE WITH THESE PEOPLE/SITUATIONS...

AMEN.

DATE

TODAY'S BIBLE READING...

THE VERSE THAT STOOD OUT MOST...

SOMETHING I CAN LEARN FROM TODAY'S READING...

WHAT
THIS
PASSAGE
SAYS
ABOUT
GOD...

ALL SCRIPTURE IS BREATHED OUT BY GOD
AND PROFITABLE FOR TEACHING, FOR
REPROOF, FOR CORRECTION, AND FOR
TRAINING IN RIGHTEOUSNESS, THAT THE
MAN OF GOD MAY BE COMPLETE,
EQUIPPED FOR EVERY GOOD WORK.
-2 TIMOTHY 3:16-17

TODAY'S CHALLENGE

DEAR GOD,

THANK YOU FOR...

GUIDE ME TODAY AS I...

HELP ME WHEN I AM TEMPTED TO...

FORGIVE ME FOR...

AS I FORGIVE...

"ASK, AND IT WILL BE GIVEN TO YOU SEEK, AND YOU WILL FIND; KNOCK, AND IT WILL BE OPENED TO YOU." -MATTHEW 7:7

BE WITH THESE PEOPLE/SITUATIONS...

AMEN.

DATE

TODAY'S BIBLE READING...

THE VERSE THAT STOOD OUT MOST...

SOMETHING I CAN LEARN FROM TODAY'S READING...

WHAT
THIS
PASSAGE
SAYS
ABOUT
GOD...

ALL SCRIPTURE IS BREATHED OUT BY GOD AND PROFITABLE FOR TEACHING, FOR REPROOF, FOR CORRECTION, AND FOR TRAINING IN RIGHTEOUSNESS, THAT THE MAN OF GOD MAY BE COMPLETE, EQUIPPED FOR EVERY GOOD WORK.
-2 TIMOTHY 3:16-17

TODAY'S CHALLENGE

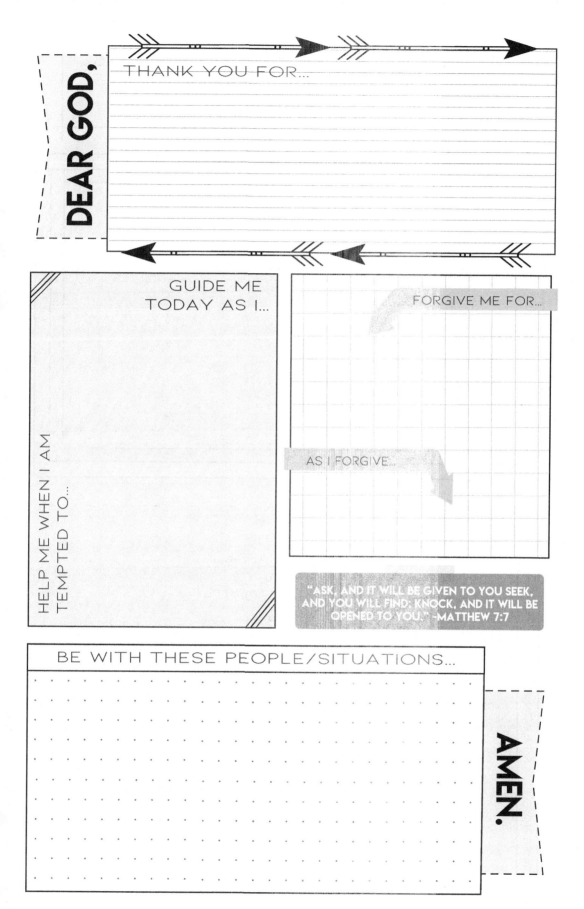

DEAR GOD,

THANK YOU FOR...

GUIDE ME TODAY AS I...

HELP ME WHEN I AM TEMPTED TO...

FORGIVE ME FOR...

AS I FORGIVE...

"ASK, AND IT WILL BE GIVEN TO YOU SEEK, AND YOU WILL FIND; KNOCK, AND IT WILL BE OPENED TO YOU." -MATTHEW 7:7

BE WITH THESE PEOPLE/SITUATIONS...

AMEN.

DATE

TODAY'S BIBLE READING...

THE VERSE THAT STOOD OUT MOST...

SOMETHING I CAN LEARN FROM TODAY'S READING...

WHAT
THIS
PASSAGE
SAYS
ABOUT
GOD...

ALL SCRIPTURE IS BREATHED OUT BY GOD
AND PROFITABLE FOR TEACHING, FOR
REPROOF, FOR CORRECTION, AND FOR
TRAINING IN RIGHTEOUSNESS, THAT THE
MAN OF GOD MAY BE COMPLETE,
EQUIPPED FOR EVERY GOOD WORK.
-2 TIMOTHY 3:16-17

TODAY'S CHALLENGE

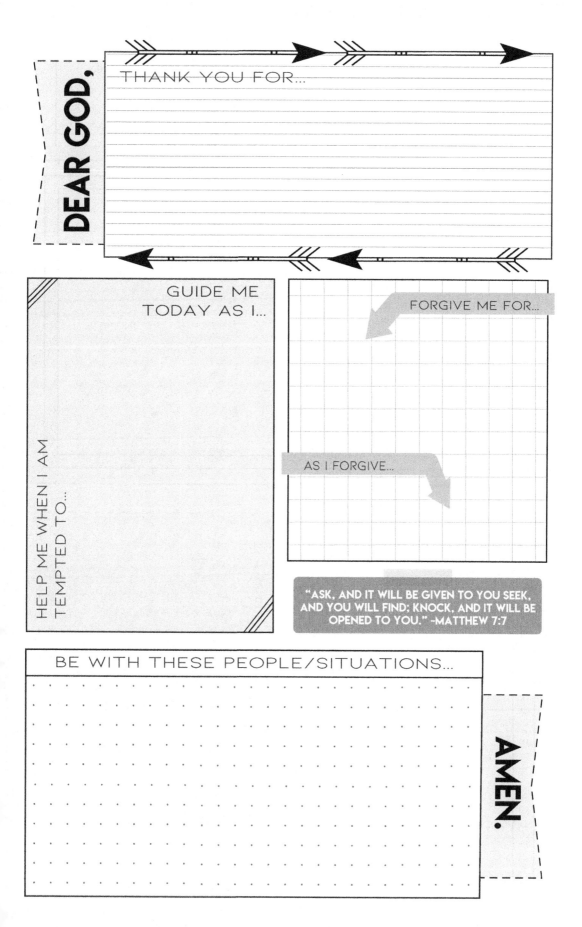

DEAR GOD,

THANK YOU FOR...

GUIDE ME TODAY AS I...

HELP ME WHEN I AM TEMPTED TO...

FORGIVE ME FOR...

AS I FORGIVE...

"ASK, AND IT WILL BE GIVEN TO YOU SEEK, AND YOU WILL FIND; KNOCK, AND IT WILL BE OPENED TO YOU." -MATTHEW 7:7

BE WITH THESE PEOPLE/SITUATIONS...

AMEN.

TODAY'S BIBLE READING...

THE VERSE THAT STOOD OUT MOST...

SOMETHING I CAN LEARN FROM TODAY'S READING...

WHAT
THIS
PASSAGE
SAYS
ABOUT
GOD...

ALL SCRIPTURE IS BREATHED OUT BY GOD AND PROFITABLE FOR TEACHING, FOR REPROOF, FOR CORRECTION, AND FOR TRAINING IN RIGHTEOUSNESS, THAT THE MAN OF GOD MAY BE COMPLETE, EQUIPPED FOR EVERY GOOD WORK.
-2 TIMOTHY 3:16-17

TODAY'S CHALLENGE

DEAR GOD,

THANK YOU FOR...

GUIDE ME TODAY AS I...

HELP ME WHEN I AM TEMPTED TO...

FORGIVE ME FOR...

AS I FORGIVE...

"ASK, AND IT WILL BE GIVEN TO YOU SEEK, AND YOU WILL FIND; KNOCK, AND IT WILL BE OPENED TO YOU." -MATTHEW 7:7

BE WITH THESE PEOPLE/SITUATIONS...

AMEN.

TODAY'S BIBLE READING...

THE VERSE THAT STOOD OUT MOST...

SOMETHING I CAN LEARN FROM TODAY'S READING...

WHAT
THIS
PASSAGE
SAYS
ABOUT
GOD...

ALL SCRIPTURE IS BREATHED OUT BY GOD AND PROFITABLE FOR TEACHING, FOR REPROOF, FOR CORRECTION, AND FOR TRAINING IN RIGHTEOUSNESS, THAT THE MAN OF GOD MAY BE COMPLETE, EQUIPPED FOR EVERY GOOD WORK.
-2 TIMOTHY 3:16-17

TODAY'S CHALLENGE

DEAR GOD,

THANK YOU FOR...

GUIDE ME
TODAY AS I...

HELP ME WHEN I AM
TEMPTED TO...

FORGIVE ME FOR...

AS I FORGIVE...

"ASK, AND IT WILL BE GIVEN TO YOU SEEK,
AND YOU WILL FIND; KNOCK, AND IT WILL BE
OPENED TO YOU." -MATTHEW 7:7

BE WITH THESE PEOPLE/SITUATIONS...

AMEN.

DATE

THE VERSE THAT STOOD OUT MOST...

SOMETHING I CAN LEARN FROM TODAY'S READING...

WHAT
THIS
PASSAGE
SAYS
ABOUT
GOD...

ALL SCRIPTURE IS BREATHED OUT BY GOD
AND PROFITABLE FOR TEACHING, FOR
REPROOF, FOR CORRECTION, AND FOR
TRAINING IN RIGHTEOUSNESS, THAT THE
MAN OF GOD MAY BE COMPLETE,
EQUIPPED FOR EVERY GOOD WORK.
-2 TIMOTHY 3:16-17

TODAY'S CHALLENGE

DEAR GOD,

THANK YOU FOR...

GUIDE ME TODAY AS I...

HELP ME WHEN I AM TEMPTED TO...

FORGIVE ME FOR...

AS I FORGIVE...

"ASK, AND IT WILL BE GIVEN TO YOU SEEK, AND YOU WILL FIND; KNOCK, AND IT WILL BE OPENED TO YOU." -MATTHEW 7:7

BE WITH THESE PEOPLE/SITUATIONS...

AMEN.

TODAY'S BIBLE READING...

THE VERSE THAT STOOD OUT MOST...

SOMETHING I CAN LEARN FROM TODAY'S READING...

WHAT
THIS
PASSAGE
SAYS
ABOUT
GOD...

ALL SCRIPTURE IS BREATHED OUT BY GOD AND PROFITABLE FOR TEACHING, FOR REPROOF, FOR CORRECTION, AND FOR TRAINING IN RIGHTEOUSNESS, THAT THE MAN OF GOD MAY BE COMPLETE, EQUIPPED FOR EVERY GOOD WORK.
-2 TIMOTHY 3:16-17

TODAY'S CHALLENGE

DEAR GOD,

THANK YOU FOR...

GUIDE ME TODAY AS I...

HELP ME WHEN I AM TEMPTED TO...

FORGIVE ME FOR...

AS I FORGIVE...

"ASK, AND IT WILL BE GIVEN TO YOU SEEK, AND YOU WILL FIND; KNOCK, AND IT WILL BE OPENED TO YOU." -MATTHEW 7:7

BE WITH THESE PEOPLE/SITUATIONS...

AMEN.

DATE

TODAY'S BIBLE READING...

THE VERSE THAT STOOD OUT MOST...

SOMETHING I CAN LEARN FROM TODAY'S READING...

WHAT
THIS
PASSAGE
SAYS
ABOUT
GOD...

ALL SCRIPTURE IS BREATHED OUT BY GOD AND PROFITABLE FOR TEACHING, FOR REPROOF, FOR CORRECTION, AND FOR TRAINING IN RIGHTEOUSNESS, THAT THE MAN OF GOD MAY BE COMPLETE, EQUIPPED FOR EVERY GOOD WORK.
-2 TIMOTHY 3:16-17

TODAY'S CHALLENGE

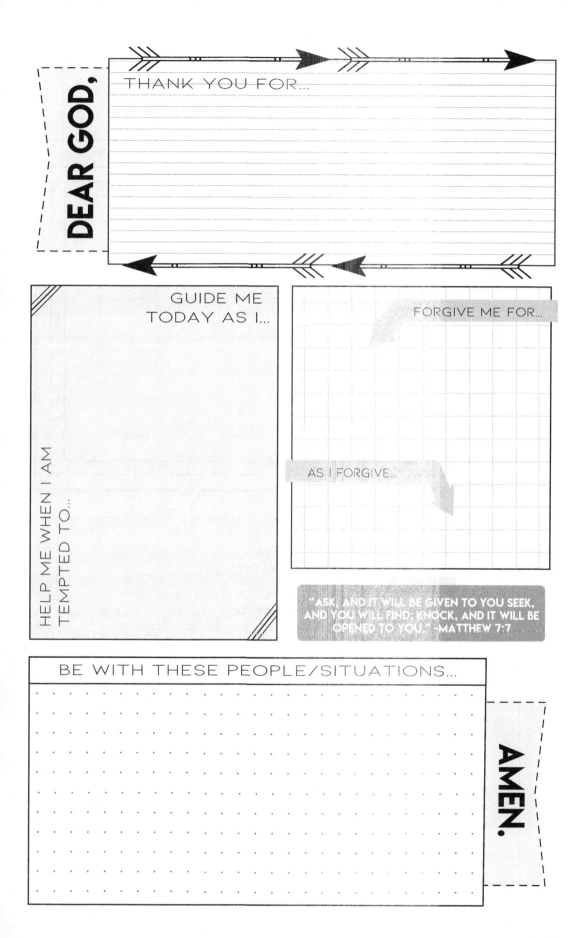

DEAR GOD,

THANK YOU FOR...

GUIDE ME TODAY AS I...

HELP ME WHEN I AM TEMPTED TO...

FORGIVE ME FOR...

AS I FORGIVE...

"ASK, AND IT WILL BE GIVEN TO YOU SEEK, AND YOU WILL FIND; KNOCK, AND IT WILL BE OPENED TO YOU." -MATTHEW 7:7

BE WITH THESE PEOPLE/SITUATIONS...

AMEN.

TODAY'S BIBLE READING...

THE VERSE THAT STOOD OUT MOST...

SOMETHING I CAN LEARN FROM TODAY'S READING...

WHAT
THIS
PASSAGE
SAYS
ABOUT
GOD...

ALL SCRIPTURE IS BREATHED OUT BY GOD AND PROFITABLE FOR TEACHING, FOR REPROOF, FOR CORRECTION, AND FOR TRAINING IN RIGHTEOUSNESS, THAT THE MAN OF GOD MAY BE COMPLETE, EQUIPPED FOR EVERY GOOD WORK. -2 TIMOTHY 3:16-17

TODAY'S CHALLENGE

DEAR GOD,

THANK YOU FOR...

GUIDE ME
TODAY AS I...

HELP ME WHEN I AM
TEMPTED TO...

FORGIVE ME FOR...

AS I FORGIVE...

"ASK, AND IT WILL BE GIVEN TO YOU SEEK, AND YOU WILL FIND; KNOCK, AND IT WILL BE OPENED TO YOU." -MATTHEW 7:7

BE WITH THESE PEOPLE/SITUATIONS...

AMEN.

TODAY'S BIBLE READING...

THE VERSE THAT STOOD OUT MOST...

SOMETHING I CAN LEARN FROM TODAY'S READING...

WHAT
THIS
PASSAGE
SAYS
ABOUT
GOD...

ALL SCRIPTURE IS BREATHED OUT BY GOD
AND PROFITABLE FOR TEACHING, FOR
REPROOF, FOR CORRECTION, AND FOR
TRAINING IN RIGHTEOUSNESS, THAT THE
MAN OF GOD MAY BE COMPLETE,
EQUIPPED FOR EVERY GOOD WORK.
-2 TIMOTHY 3:16-17

TODAY'S CHALLENGE

DEAR GOD,

THANK YOU FOR...

GUIDE ME TODAY AS I...

HELP ME WHEN I AM TEMPTED TO...

FORGIVE ME FOR...

AS I FORGIVE...

"ASK, AND IT WILL BE GIVEN TO YOU SEEK, AND YOU WILL FIND; KNOCK, AND IT WILL BE OPENED TO YOU." -MATTHEW 7:7

BE WITH THESE PEOPLE/SITUATIONS...

AMEN.

DATE

TODAY'S BIBLE READING...

THE VERSE THAT STOOD OUT MOST...

SOMETHING I CAN LEARN FROM TODAY'S READING...

WHAT
THIS
PASSAGE
SAYS
ABOUT
GOD...

ALL SCRIPTURE IS BREATHED OUT BY GOD AND PROFITABLE FOR TEACHING, FOR REPROOF, FOR CORRECTION, AND FOR TRAINING IN RIGHTEOUSNESS, THAT THE MAN OF GOD MAY BE COMPLETE, EQUIPPED FOR EVERY GOOD WORK.
-2 TIMOTHY 3:16-17

TODAY'S CHALLENGE

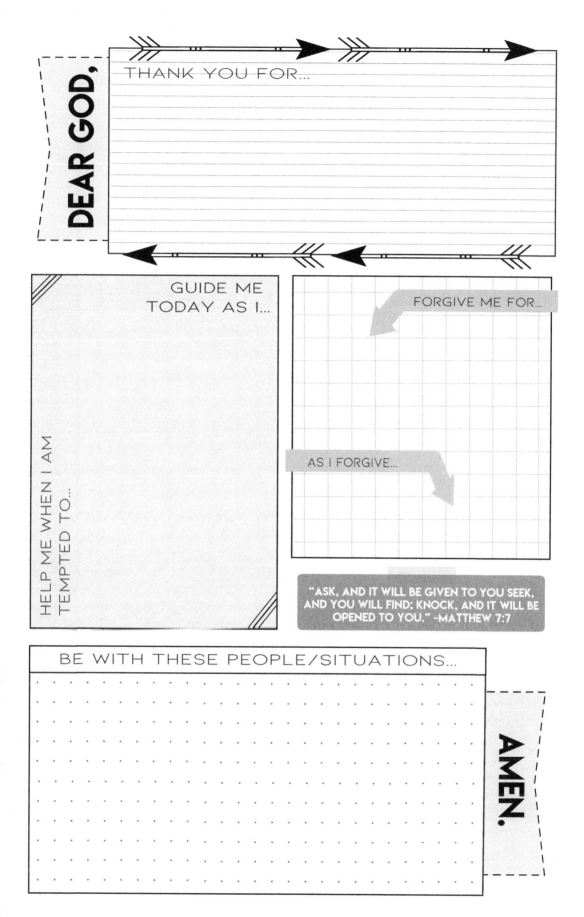

DEAR GOD,

THANK YOU FOR...

GUIDE ME TODAY AS I...

HELP ME WHEN I AM TEMPTED TO...

FORGIVE ME FOR...

AS I FORGIVE...

"ASK, AND IT WILL BE GIVEN TO YOU SEEK, AND YOU WILL FIND; KNOCK, AND IT WILL BE OPENED TO YOU." –MATTHEW 7:7

BE WITH THESE PEOPLE/SITUATIONS...

AMEN.

NOTES

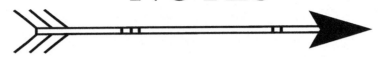

NOTES

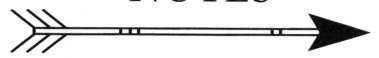

NOTES

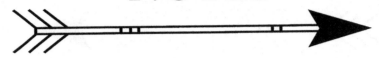

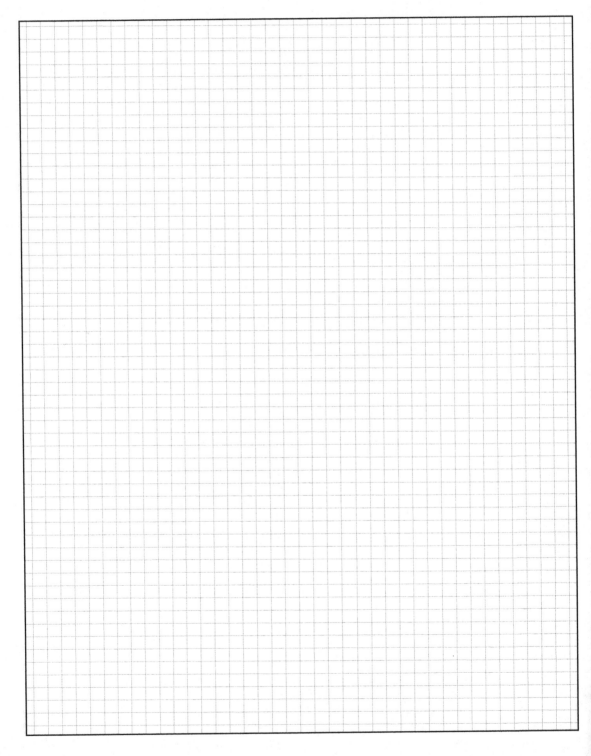

NOTES

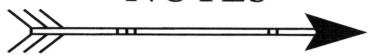

NOTES

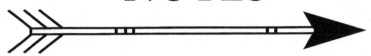

NOTES

NOTES

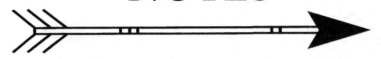

NOTES

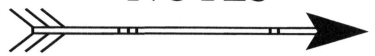

Made in the USA
Middletown, DE
13 May 2023

29940115R00040